Dearest *Nan* ... ght.
may you alw ... ght.
embraced by the ...
Renie S. Englander

Word to Image

Musings on the Hebrew Alphabet

Art and Poetry by

Renée S. Englander

To Leo Manso who unfurled my wings.
To Meredith Rosier who guided my flight.

First United States edition published by Menschette Publications

WORD to IMAGE, Musings on the Hebrew Alphabet copyright © 2018
by Renée S. Englander

Library of Congress Cataloging-in-Publication Data
Englander, Renée S.
Word to Image, Musings on the Hebrew Alphabet
ISBN: 978-0-692-19697-7

Book Design and art photography by Lydia AFIA, Emerald MUSE Inc.

Contents

Artist's Statement

My purpose is to abstract the soul essence from a word, a feeling, an object. As I work, personal meaning evolves into full expression through line, shape, color and movement. My hand and heart journey together across the page with navigational input from my head. Unlikely colors are juxtaposed to achieve interesting effects. Gestures react to one another bringing the composition to fruition. Many times I will add a texture to enhance the work. It is exciting to explore the qualities particular to pastels combining them with other materials to produce surprising results.

Biography

Renée S. Englander is an abstract painter actively exploring the essense of objective and subjective realities. She began as a painter of realistic subjects over four decades with much success. After seven years she found that she could not express herself fully and entered the world of abstract art where her love of color, pattern, and texture came together. Her studies at the Art Students League in New York City and The Woodstock School of Art have had the most profound influence on her work. Renée continues to exhibit in juried shows and solo exhibitions.A highlight of her career was to exhibit at Biennale Internazionale Dell'Arte Contemporanea in Florence, Italy.

The Artist's Pastel and Print Collection

For additional information regarding the purchase of any of the images contained in this book, please contact:

Renée S. Englander

reneeenglander37@gmail.com.

I Love A Mystery

A bit of mystery, a bit of magic, a lot of mystical power melded to produce the Hebrew alphabet.

A legend is told about a village being devastated by a drought. The inhabitants met in the synagogue praying that their lot would change. Among the villagers was a simple shepherd boy. The only thing he knew how to read was the Hebrew alphabet. The intensity of feeling in the synagogue was mounting and the boy wanted to pray but he did not know how. He opened the prayer book to the first page and began to recite all of the letters of the alphabet. He then called out to G-d: "This is all I can do, G-d. You know how the prayers should be pronounced. Please, arrange the letters in the proper way." This simple prayer resounded powerfully within the Heavens. It started to rain. The drought was over. The village was granted blessings and good fortune.

The letters of many languages form words and are a guide to pronunciation. Hebrew letters are more complex, each bearing an individual essence. To discover the essence of each letter one takes a personal journey along many different routes.

One route considers the shape of the Hebrew letters. Some shapes are playful, some strong. Beit is the second letter of the alphabet pronounced "bee". The shape (ב) is solid and often assigned the word "house." It is imagined as a house on a solid foundation. After exploring the many levels of interpretations of the letter, I believe beit to be a three sided container pouring forth blessings. On the other hand, lamed, pronounced "el," (ל) the twelfth letter of the alphabet is softer and symbolizes learning. It is the tallest letter perhaps acting as a beacon of knowledge. Its undulating shape can represent the constant change occurring during learning which resonates with me.

Another route to understanding the Hebrew letters is through gematria – a system of assigning each letter a numerical value. Words that have the same numerical value have a connection. One such example is the word Elohim which is one of the names of G-d. It has the same numerical value as Tevah, the Hebrew word for nature. Both equal 86. This connection gives much food for thought.

There are many more levels to explore in interpreting Hebrew letters. I took this journey pondering each letter in its many aspects attempting to abstract the soul essence of each letter creating a painting and accompanying haiku for each. Hebrew letters are indeed a mystery to be investigated but never accorded a universal solution.

ALEPH
Boundless

Boundlessness is shattered
Great Spirit creates all
Stars appear.

BET
Blessings

Fecund universe
Birthed blessings covering all
Many await you.

Renée S. Englander

GIMMEL
Generosity

An open hand
Eternal fountain of light
Enough for all.

DALET
Doorway

An invitation
Inner light will show the path
Fear not to enter.

HAY
Emergence

Throw off binding ties
Opportunities await
Emerge into you.

VAV
Connection

Above to below
Golden threads are created
Connections are formed.

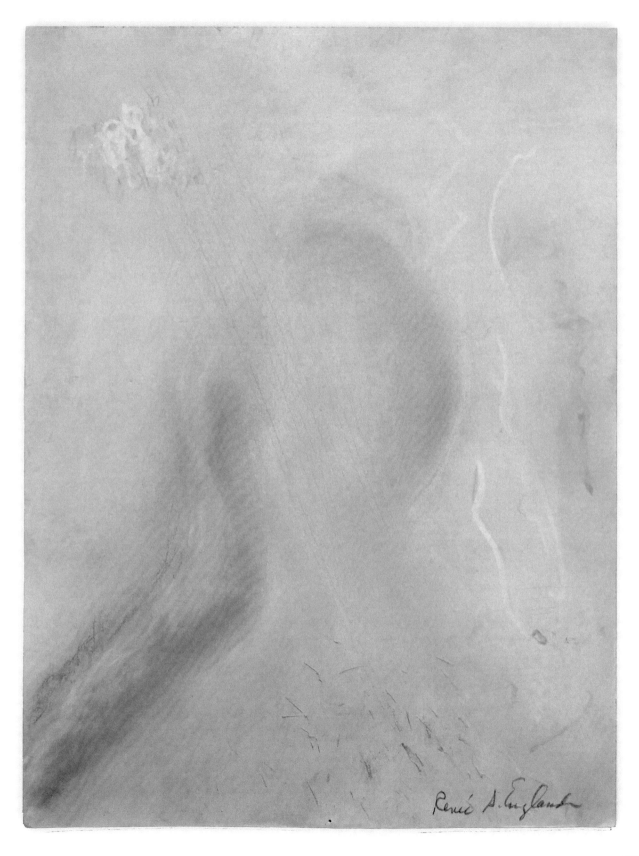

René A. England

ZAYIN
Remember

Past thoughts flood the mind
Some are soft edged and some hard.
Remember soft times.

CHET
Life

In every one
The impregnable soul
Life imbues each.

TET
Good

Turn to face the sun
Bask in the heavenly light
Goodness envelopes.

YUD
Joining

Each is separate
Holy call summons all forth
The circle is closed.

KAF
Possibilities

Palms press together
Prayers are activated
Blessings are bestowed.

LAMED
Teach

A cache of knowledge
Locked away in vault of mind
Teacher sets it free.

MEM
Waters

In the dark womb
Living waters surround you
Drink deeply.

NUN
Fish

The fish swims calmly
In its own environment
Eyes always open.

SAMECH
Inseparable

They intertwine
Cleave one to the other
They are total.

AYIN
Salvation

Lift your eyes skyward
See new possibilities
And be comforted.

PEH
Speech

Butterflies alight
Fluttering life's vibrations
Praise sounds forth.

TZADEE
Righteous

She arises
She walks in righteousness
Let her guide you.

KOF
Holiness

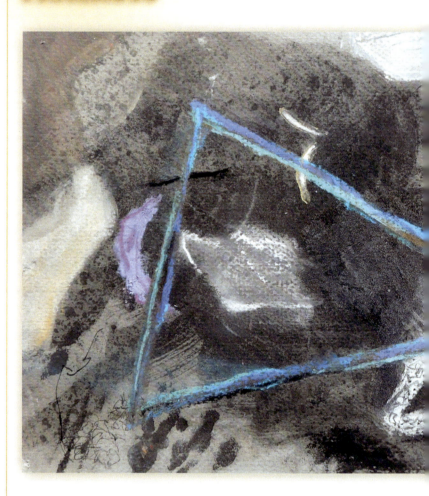

Darkness surrounds
Search for golden sparks within
Find liberation.

RESH
Redemption

Who judged them guilty?
They atone. Are they redeemed?
Does the bird fly free?

45

SHIN
Safety

You are protected
Be enfolded in mighty wings
Danger thwarted.

47

TAV
Completion

Falsehoods dissolve.
Reality issues forth
Truth seals the contract.